THE
CIVIL WAR ART OF KEITH ROCCO

First published in the United States of America in 2009 by Crimson Books, Inc.
440 Thomas Avenue, Forest Park, IL, 60130, USA
www.crimsonbooksinc.com

ISBN-13: 978-0-9841652-0-9

Edited by Lynda Fitzgerald
Print Management and Design by HeuleGordon, Inc.
Printed and bound in China

INTRODUCTION

The Civil War is the definitive American experience. No one who reads of those tumultuous years comes away without a deeper appreciation for the sacrifices that were made to shape our nation's destiny. That terrible war continues to seize the imagination and compels us to read, study, even venture to the battlefields to gain a better understanding of what happened and why. Through a variety of media we seek ways to reach into the past. Books, magazines, videos, documentaries and movies all seek to feed the demand for more.

One of the reasons that the Civil War has become such a passionate study is the photographic legacy left behind; haunting photographs of young lads, innocents being led to the slaughter; horrible images of the aftermath of battle; the slain laying in rows awaiting burial; piles of dead artillery horses lying on the battlefield; the charred remains of Atlanta, Columbia, Charleston and Richmond. All speak to us across the expanse of time. But photography can only accomplish so much. The eye needs more to feed the imagination. For this we have the painter's art.

During the war combat correspondents were accompanied by artists such as Winslow Homer, Alfred Waud, James Taylor and others who, through the power of their sketches, were able to bring the action and the drama of the battlefields and campaigns into every home. Today's media overload was not a problem in the mid-nineteenth century. People hungered for these images. Woodcut engravings and sketches were able to provide action images that were beyond the grasp of a camera.

All of these media brought the war home, but none were capable of capturing the drama and the feeling of being there that a color painting provides. With a brush stroke here and a flourish there, an artist can breathe life and emotion into the still figures on canvas. Winslow Homer, one of the best war correspondent-artists, was able to capture the experience of the soldiers he painted and his depictions of the everyday life of the soldier are

national treasures. They are windows to the past from an eyewitness. Conrad Wise Chapman provided similar images from the Confederate point of view.

Civil War art was popular during and after the war. This was especially true in the years of reconciliation and celebration. Forgetting the causes and the emotions that led to the mammoth bloodletting, artists were able to present the heroes and the spectacle of the war. Larger than life portraits of the generals and the battles abound. The vast popularity of artistic prints, tobacco cards and cyclorama's after the war, and the continued popularity of the grand spectacles of battle as portrayed by Currier & Ives and Kurz & Allison, speak to the truth of this phenomenon. But it is the realistic portrayals of the era that are most interesting and compelling. Artists of the realist school specialized in reproducing unforgettable persons and moments of history. Paul Philippoteaux produced the magnificent Gettysburg Cyclorama, which still draws crowds of spectators. Such panoramic and dramatic depictions compel viewers to stand in awe at the grand display and the Cyclorama was just one of many such spectacular works of art.

The popularity of Civil War art has not abated with the passing of the years. From Howard Pyle, Gilbert Gaul and N.C. Wyeth to the present day, Civil War art continues to capture the imagination of those who love both history and art, and have a desire to envision the breadth and scope of the war.

One of the leading artists in the field today is Keith Rocco. Keith, a student of Wyeth, Gaul, and French artist Alphonse-Marie-Adolphe de Neuville, is an internationally recognized historical artist. His work graces the walls of the Pentagon, the U.S. Army War College, the National Guard Heritage Collection, the Andrew Mellon Foundation, as well as numerous prestigious museums across the United States and in Europe. His artwork can be seen at many national battlefield parks and other historic sites and in private collections. Vast murals hang in the Wisconsin Veteran's Museum in Madison and the Museum of the Civil War Soldier in Petersburg, Virginia. Two of his paintings were commissioned for the Abraham Lincoln Museum in Springfield, Illinois. Rocco's art has been featured in numerous historical magazines and periodicals, and as cover art for dozens of books. All of this attention is no accident.

Keith Rocco's style and vision captures the look, feel and emotion of the artists of days gone by. His work is about soldiers and fighting men, in everyday life as well as the midst of battle. Though there are heroic figures and glorious moments in his art, these are happenstance, serving as a backdrop to the experience of human beings. Though his paintings are meticulously researched for accuracy insofar as details of terrain, uniforms and equipment, these are never the focus of the work, merely adornments adding depth to the portrayal of the action. One sees the past when looking at Rocco's work. The viewer is draw into the canvas, gaining an incomparable understanding of the action. No other contemporary artist is able to capture this effect as well as Keith Rocco.

Keith has had a lifelong passion for history, painting and historical artifacts that translates to the canvas. With his knowledge of the heft and texture of the items he paints, he is able to portray them as functional parts of the fighting man. The artifacts speak to the artist, providing understanding on an intuitive level. Rocco's vast personal knowledge of the subject matter helps inspire him to understand how to depict an historical event or personage.

For more than twenty years it has been my pleasure to work with Keith. At various times I have modeled, conducted research, and provided narratives for his artwork. I have accompanied him on research trips and to visit battlefields, thereby gaining insight into his talent and methodology. Finding the right words to describe the events in his paintings has been both rewarding and

challenging. My own interest, both in the history and art has benefited immensely from this relationship. Keith and I share a common passion for history and historical artifacts. The fact that we both perceive the real story of the war to be that of the individuals that fought it adds to the impact of the experience.

In this volume, some of Rocco's signature pieces are presented with all new text. Additionally, many of the works here are previously unpublished. The Civil War Art of Keith Rocco is a treasure trove of the artist's work, presenting a soldier's view of the experience of the Civil War.

Robert I. Girardi

The advent of the Civil War was an exciting time for the youth of the Northern and Southern States. After the surrender of Fort Sumter in April, 1861, the youths of both sides flocked to the colors, eager to prove their worth on the battlefield. Boastful youngsters primed on the heroic deeds of their Revolutionary War ancestors, or schooled with ideas of gallantry of the knights as portrayed by Sir Walter Scott were eager to go on their own quests, to fight for the Union or for their rights. A young man who did not volunteer was likely to receive disapproving looks from local young ladies. Some who did not rush to the ranks received petticoats in the mail as a sign of their lack of masculine virtues. The others flocked to the ranks, eager to see the elephant, or to get a red badge of courage, an honorable wound. War was a grand adventure that nobody wanted to miss out on. So many volunteers rose up in response to Abraham Lincoln's call for 75,000 volunteers that some Northern governors were forced to turn them away. There simply weren't enough rifles and uniforms to equip them. Some of the volunteers feared that the war would end before they got the opportunity to get into the fight. The new recruits marched off, carrying banners sewn by their mothers and sweethearts, among a panoply of rousing patriotic music, parades and stirring speeches.

Such youthful naïveté swelled the ranks of both armies. Photographs of the early war volunteers show young lads dressed up in soldier's clothes, often sporting pistols and knives and striking fierce poses for the camera. The innocence and zeal in their eyes speaks volumes.

As young recruits enlisted, they soon were subjected to the growing pains brought about by army rules, regulations and routine. No glory could be earned until the youths were properly schooled. Excitement gave way to drudgery in the daily routine of guard duty, drill, fatigue duty, drill and even more drill. Ralsa Rice, of Ohio, recalled, "While in camp we were kept constantly employed learning the business of soldiering. The transition from civilian to soldier we found did not consist wholly in donning a uniform…" The youths grumbled about drilling, grumbled about the rules and grumbled about having to do labor—gathering wood and water, digging latrines or trenches did not appeal to their martial ardor. They enlisted to fight, not work. Slowly, but surely, however, the transition from civilian to soldier did occur. In just a few months, the green youths had turned into cogs in a fighting machine.

Private Columbus Taylor, as depicted in the painting,

enlisted in Co D, 3rd Georgia Volunteer Infantry. The 3rd Georgia was organized in April 1861 for one year and was stationed at Portsmouth, Virginia, seeing action in the early campaigns on the east coast. In the Spring of 1862 the regiment was reorganized for an additional two years service and became part of the Army of Northern Virginia, remaining with that army until the surrender at Appomattox Courthouse in April 1865. During its period of service, the 3rd Georgia fought in some fifty battles.

Taylor is a dapper looking young Confederate, clad in an early war uniform from Georgia, including the Georgia state belt buckle. Keith Rocco has captured the essence of this youth from a famous wartime photograph. Taylor's face still shows lingering traces of the innocence of the new recruit, but he is partially broken in by some field experience here in the Winter of 1861-62. Taylor is dressed warmly in his greatcoat as he sips from a cup of coffee—a luxury soon he will soon be forced to live without. He stands grasping his musket. His cartridge box is worn on the outside of the coat, which was customary. He has a look of confidence, but not the jauntiness of a veteran, about him as he stands on picket duty in the woods. Taylor was killed in action with many of his pards on July 1, 1862 during the Battle of Malvern Hill.

3RD GEORGIA PRIVATE.

12" X 9"

The Battle of Bull Run, or Manassas, was the great awakening for both sides in the Civil War. Flush with their victory, the Confederates were convinced that they could fight a successful war. Humiliated by the defeat, the Union regrouped its army and readied itself for a long ordeal. The battle was a baptism of fire for both sides. Heroes and martyrs abounded on either side. Legends were made. One became immortal.

July 21st of 1861 would be an important day in the life of Brigadier General Thomas Jonathan Jackson. His brigade of Virginians was poised on the reverse slope of Henry House Hill. A series of Federal attacks on the position had been beaten back, with heavy casualties on both sides. Jackson steadied his men as they endured a bombardment of Federal artillery preparatory to another grand assault up the slopes of the hill.

Jackson was no stranger to combat. Schooled at West Point, he had served with distinction in the artillery service during the Mexican War. Yet Jackson left the army in the years before the Civil War. He became extremely devout and rigid in his beliefs and personal behavior. When he took a professorship at Virginia Military Institute, his strict discipline and unimaginative instruction led his students to christen him "Tom Fool."

Jackson returned to the army to fight for the Confederacy at the beginning of the war and was assigned to a regimental

command. He drilled his men proficiently and was quickly promoted to brigade command. His regiments, the 2nd, 4th, 5th, 27th and 33rd Virginia, were aware that their commander was no fool, and this day he had been given a new nickname. During a crisis in the battle, as the beaten men of General Barnard Bee's brigade fell back, Bee saw the resolute Jackson, seemingly unperturbed by the flow of the battle. Bee told Jackson that the Federals were beating them back. "Then, sir, we will give them the bayonet!" Bee, perhaps agitated by the losses in his brigade, was strengthened by this response. "There is Jackson standing like a stone wall!" Bee exclaimed to his troops, "Rally behind the Virginians!" Bee fell, mortally wounded, but his last words became immortal. "Stonewall" Jackson was christened.

In the crisis of the battle, as the Federals made another grand assault on Henry House Hill, Jackson was encouraging and instructing his men. "Reserve your fire until they come within fifty yards," he ordered, then "give them the bayonet." For emphasis he also told them that when they charged, they were to "yell like furies."

The Virginians rose up to the crest of the hill and fired several devastating volleys into the faces of the attacking Federals. Then, Jackson led his brigade in a counterattack which broke the Federal assault and captured Rickett's battery of artillery which had advanced to provide close support for the Federal infantry attack. Fighting over the battery was intense, with each side giving and retaking lost ground. But Jackson's charge blunted the Union assault and swung the tide of the battle in favor of the Confederacy. Though fierce fighting continued, the Federals lost confidence. An infusion of fresh troops into the fight proved decisive for the Southern army, and the Federals fled in panic.

Keith Rocco shows Jackson in his splendor, mounted on his war horse, leading his brigade into action as artillery shells burst overhead. The fighting men are seen in early war uniforms. Some sport havelocks to protect themselves from the sun. Company guidons mark regimental fronts. Jackson sits on his horse calmly, looking steadfastly forward as he leads his brigade to victory.

BAPTISM AT MANASSAS

PRIVATE COLLECTION

16" X 24"

LOUISIANA TIGERS

One of the most colorful and infamous Civil War regiments was the Louisiana Tigers. First organized in New Orleans, the Tigers were commanded by the no less colorful Roberdeau Wheat. Though the designation "Louisiana Tigers" originated with Company B of Wheat's Battalion, the name would grow to encompass the entire brigade.

The original Tigers were comprised of "the very dregs of the city," and represented a variety of ethnicities and occupations from the streets and wharves of New Orleans. An ethnic mix of two dozen nationalities, including Irish dock workers (wharf rats) and other waterfront types, as well as a mix of Frenchmen and Chinese, gave the Tigers a distinctively alien character. Recruits included veterans of the Mexican War, various state militia units and the participants in the filibustering efforts in Central America. The recruits were reputedly denizens of the many barrooms, brothels, jailhouses and included pimps, lawyers and thieves among their numbers.

Major Chatham Roberdeau Wheat, a native of Virginia, had a colorful career. He was a lawyer, politician, soldier, and a renowned filibusterer. As a soldier, he fought in the Mexican war, and with William Walker in Central America and Giuseppe Garibaldi in Italy. Wheat was instrumental in raising and equipping the five company battalion that became the Tigers. Despite his efforts Wheat was not rewarded with a commission as general. His men were just too ill-disciplined.

The Tigers were a Zouave regiment and were colorfully dressed in a uniform consisting of straw hats or a scarlet skull cap with blue tassels, blue and white striped socks and pants, white leggings and loose fitting dark blue jackets with red trim. Many of the men wore emblazoned slogans on their hats, such as "Tiger by Nature."

The men were armed with the Enfield rifle-musket. Many sported the long handled Bowie knives which they were not afraid to wield with effect and which added to their reputation for ferocity. Harper's Weekly claimed that the Tigers, "dig up the corpses of our dead soldiers, and send their bones home to their lady loves as trophies…" and were "capable of assassinating a Union man or of whipping a black woman to death…"

The hard fighting reputation of the Tigers was earned at the first battle of Bull Run, where they held the left flank of the Confederate line on Matthews Hill. The Tigers were deployed as skirmishers and formed near the stone bridge. Despite being overwhelmingly outnumbered, the Tigers and another regiment of Colonel Nathan G. Evans' brigade held their position for several hours. Wheat was seriously wounded. Despite the uneven numbers, Evans ordered an attack on the advancing Union division, commanded by Daniel Tyler. Nobody ever forgot the reckless charge, which stalled the Union advance. The Tigers rushed into the fight brandishing and using their fearsome Bowie knives. Their reputation was made.

In addition to their penchant for hard fighting in combat, the unit was also known for thievery, hard drinking and general rowdiness if not downright criminal behavior. William McClendon of the 15th Alabama Infantry was actually afraid of the Tigers, writing that he feared he would encounter them somewhere and that they would "knock me down and stamp me half to death," like they did to a friend of his.

In 1862, Wheat's Tigers were assigned to the Louisiana brigade commanded by Brigadier General Richard Taylor and attached to the army commanded by Stonewall Jackson, then operating in the Shenandoah Valley. The battalion took a prominent role in the battles of Front Royal, Winchester and Port Republic. When Jackson brought his forces to join the Army of Northern Virginia, the Tigers accompanied him. They fought in the Seven Days' battles around Richmond, where their gallant leader Wheat was mortally wounded at the Battle of Gaines Mill. Wheat had a legendary career and died as befits a legend, uttering his last words, "Bury me on the field, boys."

The Tigers survived under other guises and other commanders. The name grew to embrace the entire brigade, which fought to the end of the war, fighting with aplomb at Antietam, Fredericksburg, Gettysburg, Rappahannock Station and Spotsylvania. The few remnants ultimately surrendered at Appomattox Court House. Throughout the war the Tigers maintained their reputation, earning immortality as a unit.

The Tigers are depicted in their original uniforms, loading and firing as skirmishers, looking every bit as fierce as their reputation warranted.

In the spring of 1862 the Army of the Potomac, commanded by Major General George B. McClellan, had advanced up the peninsula between the York and James Rivers and was threatening the safety of the Confederate capital of Richmond, Virginia. Contesting McClellan was the Army of Northern Virginia, now commanded by General Robert E. Lee. Under Lee, the Confederates were not about to wait for the Federals to conduct a formal siege of the city. Lee was audacious and went on the offensive in a series of battles known as the Seven Days', successfully driving the Union from the gates of Richmond.

On June 27, at Gaines Mill the two armies clashed in one of the most important of these battles. The Union V Corps, commanded by Major General Fitz John Porter, had blunted Confederate attacks all day, from a nearly impregnable position behind barricades atop a hill. Porter was buying time for McClellan to move the bulk of his army. By late afternoon, the Confederates were tired, but ready for one final effort.

A fresh Confederate division arrived under William H.C. Whiting, consisting of two brigades. The brigades were Colonel Evander Law's brigade: the 2nd and 11th Mississippi, 4th Alabama, and the 6th North Carolina, and Brigadier General John B. Hood's Texas Brigade: the 1st, 4th and 5th Texas, 18th Georgia and the Hampton Legion from South Carolina. These would conduct the final assault of the day. Lee himself positioned Whiting's division for the

assault. Hood's brigade would make its reputation this day with its charge into history.

Hood formed his men in an open field and rapidly advanced towards the Federals. As the brigade began taking fire the men quickened their pace. Charging through a strip of woods barely fifty yards thick, the 4th Texas and the supporting regiments splashed across Boatswain's Creek, a shallow, marshy stream with steep, slippery banks. Charging into a "very hot sheet of musketry," the regiment lost men with every step. Most of the command and field officers were killed or wounded until "every man was his own commander," according to one veteran. The charge was slowed by the dead, wounded and stragglers from previous attacks, but continued on.

The 4th Texas led the charge. Despite suffering heavy loss they reached the Union breastworks and drove the disheartened Federals out of their position, their momentum carrying them deep into the enemy's rear. When the remainder of the attackers broke through, the Union defenders fled in confusion, suffering heavily, losing many prisoners and a number of artillery pieces. The Confederate breakthrough shattered the Union line and hastened McClellan on his retreat. The immediate threat to Richmond was over. The cost had been high though. Hood's brigade lost 571 men, 253 of whom were from the 4th Texas. When he surveyed the battlefield, Stonewall Jackson remarked, "The men that carried this position were soldiers indeed!"

In the painting, two companies of the 4th Texas Infantry of Hood's Texas Brigade are shown advancing in the final attack on the Union line at Gaines Mill. The Federal fortification of logs, rocks and even their knapsacks is visible in the distance. The Confederates are shown in the woods, crossing Boatswain's Creek as they advance in the final attack. Two companies are clad in Confederate gray frockcoats. Some of the men are proudly wearing the trademark silver Texas star on their hats. In the right foreground, Lieutenant W.D. Rounsavall of Co K, the "Sandy Point Mounted Rifles," is shown encouraging a soldier, moments before being wounded. Rounsavall lost an arm at Gaines Mill. The effect of battle smoke, dampness from the swampy terrain and the last departing rays of the afternoon sun add to the dramatic effect of this painting.

GAINES MILL

30" X 44"

THE OUTPOST

oldiers typically spent thirty days in camp for each day in combat. Camp security was a vital task, performed by pickets, or outposts. Their duties included maintaining security for the encampment, concealing one's strength and position and acquiring intelligence about the enemy's strength and dispositions. As a rule, forward outposts were prepared to serve both as an early warning of an imminent enemy attack as well as a defensive perimeter for the army. The advanced guard forced an enemy to move slowly and cautiously, and in case of an attack, delayed him as long as possible. Pickets policed their own camps which both prevented unauthorized incursions as well as desertions.

According to British military expert Patrick Leonard Macdougall "the safety of an army in an enemy's country depends on the manner in which the outpost duty is performed." An officer in command of outposts ought to act "as if the safety of the whole army depended on his individual vigilance." In case of an enemy attack, the outposts would fight as skirmishers and hold their ground tenaciously, sending warning to the main body and buying time for them to form up and render support. If forced to retire, they would fall back in such a way as to concentrate their forces and rejoin the main body of troops. This duty was considered so serious, that the time-honored penalty for being caught sleeping while on sentry was death.

Picket posts were chosen carefully. Factors to be considered were proximity to the enemy, concealment, and field of view. Pickets needed to view the enemy in order to be alerted if any sudden movement or attack was underway and to immediately pass that information to their superiors while remaining undetected. Pickets probed enemy lines to uncover or capture enemy pickets and prevented the enemy from performing similar tasks. It was of paramount importance that the position selected be situated so as not to allow the enemy to approach it from a concealed position, thereby limiting the possibility of the pickets being taken by surprise.

Picket or outpost duty fell to an entire regiment for a twenty-four hour period. Men would be posted in three stations, the furthest being a mile or two from the main camp. The first line, called the Advance Picket was the outermost position and the earliest line of defense. The second line, called the Second Guard was stationed behind the advance picket. The Rear Guard, or reserves, were stationed closest to camp and were responsible to relieve or reinforce the other stations as needed. At any given time one-third of the force was on duty for a two hour shift. All intelligence gathered, persons encountered, or prisoners taken, were to be reported in detail.

Picket duty was routine and tedious and was usually grumbled at by the soldiers. Minutes passed slowly, often in unpleasant weather, but there were those with a creative or perverse frame of mind who enjoyed such duty as an opportunity to go exploring, foraging or adventure seeking. Often, pickets from both sides would declare an informal truce to trade coffee, tobacco, newspapers, boasts and lamentations. These activities were officially frowned upon but usually overlooked if kept discreet.

Many soldiers wrote of their experiences on the picket line when they were green enough to feel the full weight of their responsibility. Wilbur Fisk, of the 2nd Vermont recalled, "Of all the duties required of us, picketing is considered among the least desirable, especially so if the nights are cold and stormy… Walking back and forth on a beat alone, as we are strictly required to do, is by no means an expeditious method of killing time." Many grumbled about this duty, but some were able to see its beneficial side. Robert H. Strong, of the 105th Illinois wrote. "Nearly all of the boys liked it, as it rid us of camp duty, drilling and such. While there was some danger …we had more liberty." Depending on weather and circumstances, off duty pickets could sleep, explore the countryside, go fishing or foraging for extra food in the farms and fields nearby.

Here, veteran Federal soldiers are on the lookout in an advanced position along the trenches. Peering off into the distance they vigilantly watch for the enemy. A headlog is mounted atop two posts in the rifle pit to afford protection from enemy sharpshooters. One man watches while his partners take advantage of the opportunity to get some rest, relax and await their own turn to become the eyes of the army.

THE OUTPOST

Reconnaissance duty was performed by both infantry and cavalry, and by officers and engineer details. The purpose was to gather intelligence suitable for the authorities to make plans, operational and incidental, allowing a commander to make appropriate informed decisions both for daily operations as well as for a campaign. Information gathered might be estimates of an enemy's location, strength and purpose; it might also be practical; detailing the location of roads, bridges and river crossings and their suitability for the transport of wagons and artillery. Another purpose was to ascertain whether the resources of the area could sustain an army in the field; to assess the suitability and location of water sources, food, and other necessities and locating suitable campgrounds, for example. Some factors influencing this might be the existence of mills, sawmills, timber, railroads and storehouses. Reconnaissance might also be a means of determining enemy activity and strength, weak points in his fortifications or other vulnerabilities in his defenses and any other useful information.

Reconnaissance was especially important for Civil War armies operating in the field. Detailed maps of the country's interior were either non-existent, or wildly inaccurate and not suitable for military operations. Even by 1860 the most accurate maps were coastal surveys. The most readily available map of Virginia was dated 1827, although it had been updated in 1859. To compensate for these deficiencies, army commanders needed the assistance of local guides, engineer survey parties or a reconnaissance mission. Information could be obtained from spies, refugees, prisoners or anyone else familiar with the countryside. Personal observation, enhanced by other information was the ideal circumstance. Even a rudimentary sketch map based on a visual inspection of the terrain was better than nothing to a commander operating blind.

Officers selected for reconnaissance needed to be perceptive, knowledgeable as to the needs of the army, and able to report in an intelligent and concise manner. He should be capable of calculating distances and tolerances, and able to estimate numbers with a degree of certainty. He must have insight and imagination and the ability to quickly recognize suitable terrain for army operations. Thus equipped with the information, a commander could create a detailed military map and operate accordingly.

Many Civil War armies produced maps in the field using a photographic reproduction technique. The map was drawn on tracing paper and then covered by another sheet treated with silver nitrate. When exposed to sunlight the second sheet blackened except where the lines were drawn, and black map with white markings was created. Later in the war bases near the front were equipped with lithographic stones upon which maps could be reproduced in color or on better quality material. In 1864, as William T. Sherman advanced upon Atlanta, his officers were equipped with detailed maps on cloth. These proved resilient in the hardship of active campaigning. During the war field armies were provided with a total of 20,938 maps.

One of the most famous instances of a decisive action taken by a skilled engineer conducting reconnaissance occurred at Gettysburg. General Gouverneur K. Warren, acting as George Meade's chief engineer, was reconnoitering the Union lines and saw that Little Round Top was all but unoccupied by Union troops just as a major Confederate attack was heading that way. Warren saw that the hill was the key to the Union line and must be held at all costs. He diverted a brigade of Federal soldiers on his own authority and ordered them to hold Little Round Top. His action is credited with saving the day for the Union. The Warren monument on Little Round Top is one of the most recognizable Civil War monuments. He stands looking out across the fields, binoculars in hand.

The painting depicts two Confederate soldiers participating in an active reconnaissance, presumably in combat conditions. Crouching on the slope of a ridge in tall grass, an officer peers about. He is holding a pair of binoculars, mulling over what he sees. A trusted first sergeant is at the ready, musket loaded. He is relaxed, but vigilant, as he puffs on a favorite pipe. Both men are concealed and based on their gear, ready for anything. The painting is indicative of the importance and danger of this vital duty.

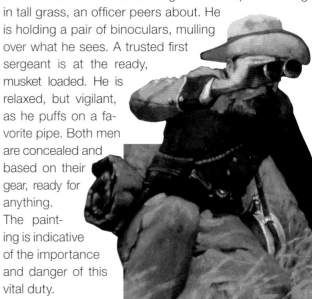

CONFEDERATE RECONNAISSANCE

FIFES AND DRUMS

Music was an important way for the army to communicate with the men in the ranks. Bugle calls and drum beats were two methods of communicating commands and orders in camp and in battle, while marching bands raised spirits and enabled soldiers to march in cadence, on the road or the parade ground.In any event, music was a constant and necessary factor in the life of Civil War armies.

The daily routine of the armies was regulated by a series of bugle calls. From reveille to tattoo, music commanded the actions of daily life in camp. There were tunes for dress parade, guard mount, colors, reviews and funerals. A variety of bugle calls sent signals to infantry, cavalry or artillery units. Each arm of the service had its own series of commands and every officer was expected to "make himself perfectly acquainted with the bugle signals, and should…be enabled, if necessary, to sound them."

On the march, a spirited tune eased the drudgery of hot, dusty roads and endless starts and stops. "By this means the men kept precise step, one soldier recalled, "it prevented the men from straggling, as they became imbued with the pride of making a soldierly display." In general, the musicians were noncombatants, though they were expected to perform fatigue duties. Drummers and buglers played music, served as stretcher and litter bearers, or as needed in moving the wounded. These latter duties included serving as assistants to surgeons performing amputations as well as gathering and burying the dead. When not performing official functions, the bands played for enjoyment and entertainment. Evening concerts were staged to amuse the troops. Serenades for officers and visiting dignitaries were common occurrences, and the strains of popular tunes could be heard long into the night. In one famous instance at Stones River, Union and Confederate bands, within hearing distance of each other, tried to out perform the other. The dueling bands simultaneously struck up "Home, Sweet Home," and all animosity faded as the soldiers of both armies lent their thoughts to loved ones.

In addition to field music, Civil War armies also had regimental and brigade bands. These were organized to provide music for events, parades, ceremonies and entertainment of the troops. Early in the war each Union regiment was authorized to have its own musicians, twenty-four men plus a drum major, and each brigade had a band of sixteen musicians plus a leader. In addition to these, each company was entitled to have a drummer and a fifer. Since they were considered non-combatants, they were exempted from many of the duties of the regular soldiers. Confederate regiments were authorized to have bands of sixteen members.

Soon the government realized that having so many men serving as musicians was an extravagant waste of manpower and actions were taken to limit the numbers allowed in bands. Regimental bands were eliminated or consolidated with brigade bands. Many bandsmen were returned to the fighting ranks. Others were discharged.

Here we see a typical fife and drum corps. Regiments thus equipped had a formal reveille every morning to the tune of fifes and drums. Each melody conveyed a specific message: first call, fall in, inspection, to arms etc. This band is in camp, as evidenced by the row of tents in the background, and are sounding one of many typical calls. The drum major stands at attention while the men pipe out the orders. The musicians are devoid of any arms or accouterments except for their instruments. It is a fitting rendition of a typical and necessary duty, a reality of life for the common soldier of the Civil War.

Sunday in Camp

Army life was one of routine, rules and work, broken up only occasionally by combat. The monotony was relieved somewhat during the off hours or on Sundays, when routine duties were minimized. There was generally a formal inspection of arms and accouterments on Sunday mornings, so care had to be taken to see that clothes were neat and tidy and that weapons and equipment were properly cleaned and maintained. Company streets were policed and no mess or untidiness was to be seen. Company officers gave the men a quick overlook before the brigade commander came by. According to Robert H. Strong of the 105th Illinois, "We had inspection of arms every Sunday…Our clothes had to be neat and tidy, our brass belt buckles and other brass polished…" The inspection officer wore white gloves and woe to the soldier who did not keep his kit properly, or who had a dirty musket.

After the formal inspection, the day was generally given to religious services and leisure activities. At such times the men were free to engage in personal pursuits such as reading the newspapers, writing home, playing games or getting their haircut. Many regiments had their own barbers or at least those who claimed to be such.

Many soldiers took advantage of the personal time to read or write letters. Such missives were treasured by the recipients. One of the most common lamentations one finds in soldier's letters is that there is never enough news from home. "This day was spent principally in our tents," wrote Aaron Dunbar of the 93rd Illinois, "reading, writing, joking, quarreling about who should go after water or get dinner, each one trying to make sure it wasn't his turn…"

Leisure time also permitted playing pranks or other hi-jinks, such as leaving canteens filled with gunpowder near campfires or throwing a live cartridge into the fire just for laughs. The more solemn types could attend church services, see a play or attend concerts. Soldiers played music, or games like baseball, which was widely popular at the time. "Camp life is not much different from what I expected," wrote Charles Haydon of the 2nd Michigan Infantry, "Card playing, profanity and the stealing of provisions are among the most noted characteristics outside of the duties…"

One favorite pastime was gambling. All sorts of games of chance were played, from poker to chuck-a-luck, or betting on lice races. "Poker was king," one soldier wrote, "a game…could be found in almost every company street." Officers as well as men were wont to play these games of chance. In the Army of Tennessee, near Chattanooga, the Confederate soldiers organized a two-acre 'Gambler's Paradise.'

Keith Rocco's painting evokes images of similar work by Winslow Homer. A group of officers sits around on a bench in camp, reading the paper and passing time while one of their pards is getting a shave from the company barber. Laughing, joking and gossiping, the scene depicts the lighter side of the all too serious war. The officers are without side-arms as reflects their off-duty status. The detail is all here, a company street of Sibley tents in the background, shaving basin and towel, even one of the men cradling his cherished pipe. All too soon duty would call again.

SUNDAY IN CAMP

The long arm of both armies was the artillery. Artillery provided armies with massed firepower and, if used effectively, could decimate an attacking force, or bombard and destroy a defensive position. At Malvern Hill, Antietam, Fredericksburg and Gettysburg, just to name four battles, artillery played a decisive role in the outcome. Confederate Major General Daniel Harvey Hill, after witnessing the carnage caused by the Federal artillery at Malvern Hill, in June 1862, remarked that it "was not war, but murder." Such was the destructive power of the field artillery in combat.

The artillery of both the Union and Confederate armies was organized into batteries of four or six guns each. Each gun was served by an eight man crew and six drivers commanded by the gunner. Each man on the crew had a specific function and all were cross-trained to fill in as circumstances warranted. Artillerists were required to know how to move, aim and fire the gun. The gunner would determine the range to the target and decide upon the type of ammunition and the appropriate time for the fuse. Other crewmen would get the ammunition, load the gun, ram the charge home and clean the muzzle for the next round. A full strength battery would consist of six guns, the accompanying limbers, caissons, forge and tools, one hundred officers and men and as many as 150 horses. With a captain in command, the battery was divided into sections of two guns each commanded by a lieutenant with each gun crew commanded by a sergeant.

"Nothing in war is more exciting than to see a battery go into action..." wrote Henry Eby, 7th Illinois Cavalry, "they will dash into the midst of the fight...and open their volcano on the enemy...It is the grandest yet most awful spectacle that war affords."

David Griffin of the 2nd Minnesota witnessed a company of artillery and wrote, "I can see them drill...They have six horses on each cannon and a rider on each high horse and six men to handle the cannon. They go through the motions of loading and firing very fast and when they wheel or go from one place to another they go on a full run." Constant drill made the gun crews proficient in being able to unlimber to go into action, or to limber to get out of harm's way, in about a minute.

It was not only the gunners who played a vital role in the artillery service, but the support crew as well. In fact, in combat conditions, it was generally more dangerous to be standing with the horses, caissons and reserve ammunition chests than it was to be serving the gun. One of the best ways to silence an enemy's guns or render them ineffective was to kill the battery's horses and target its caissons, thus rendering them impotent and immobile. One of the most famous images of the battle of Gettysburg is the heap of dead horses of the 9th Massachusetts Battery, slain in numbers as the guns tried to withdraw from the Trostle Farm.

The painting opposite depicts a Federal artillery driver holding his distinctive Grimsley artillery driver's saddle. The Grimsley saddle was adopted by the army in the 1850's. It was specifically designed and outfitted to help the driver control the horse and also pull the gun. The leather horse collar was topped with iron hames which were used to secure the traces that pulled the guns. The driver and his saddle were the key to mobility. In general, artillery pieces were pulled by six horses. The driver rode the first or lead horse on the left hand side of the team. It was his duty to control the horses and lead them into action. The driver's responsibilities, in addition to the required drill, included tending to all of the needs of his horses and seeing to their health. It was an arduous, unglamorous, but vital function.

Here, a typical Federal driver is seen standing in his red-trimmed artillery shell jacket and kepi, adorned with the crossed cannon emblem signifying artillery. He is wearing gauntlets and belt and is looking into the distance, anticipating the order to saddle up and go into action.

Image this page, courtesy National Park Service

Cavalry was the mobile branch of the military, its function to range ahead, gathering intelligence, screening the movements of an army and to make quick, powerful offensive thrusts into an enemy's territory, discovering his strength, disrupting his communications and supplies and generally wreaking havoc. Too often, especially early in the war, cavalry was used only as headquarters guards, escorts for supply trains or picket duty. Later, as the offensive striking power of the horse soldiers was realized, cavalry became a potent offensive weapon, able to cut off an enemy and fight him toe to toe until powerful infantry columns advanced. Using these tactics, General Ulysses S. Grant was able to force Robert E. Lee to surrender to end the war.

At the onset of the Civil War, Union cavalry were generally unskilled and naïve in the handling and care of horses and the rigors of the service. Farmers who could hitch a wagon and drive a plow were novices when it came to saddling and riding a horse under combat conditions. Chauncy Norton of the 15th New York cavalry remembered that "Many of them showed more fear of their horses than they ever did afterward of the enemy." It took years, rather than months, to become a veteran horse soldier.

Confederate cavalry in the early stages of the war had a decided advantage. Unlike their Union counterparts, they were responsible for providing their own horses and were already familiar with both riding and caring for their four-legged partners. This skill translated to better performance in the field, where Confederate cavaliers literally rode around the Federals. But with the passage of time this advantage faded and by 1863 the Union horse soldier was as skilled as his foe and better armed and equipped. On June 9th 1863, at Brandy Station, Virginia, 17,000 Union and Confederate soldiers engaged in the largest cavalry battle of the war. Though the battle ended as a Confederate victory, the Federal cavalry proved that they were every bit the equal of their Southern foes.

In general, life in the cavalry was more work and more action than life in the infantry. In the healthy rivalry between the services, cavalry usually came up short to derisive taunts of "Here's your mule!" or "Whoever saw a dead cavalryman?" Nonetheless cavalry saw hard service. For example, William Hyndman of the 4th Pennsylvania Cavalry recalled, "All the long, cold winter of 1862 and '63 we did picket duty almost continually…we were generally three days out and three in, in the meantime making scouts and reconnaissances. Each was seldom in camp more than a day at a time. We had a long and exposed line to guard, and had to scout the country in the vicinity of our forces, in order to guard against raids and surprises by any large body of the enemy."

Cavalry became an effective striking force behind the lines or in long ranging raids to disrupt supply lines and destroy railroads. Confederate Generals Nathan Bedford Forrest, James Ewell Brown Stuart and John Hunt Morgan became names to be dreaded by Union commanders. On the Federal side, James Harrison Wilson, John Buford and Philip H. Sheridan also led cavalry effectively, earning great renown.

Keith Rocco's painting depicts a Union first sergeant of cavalry, perhaps on a reconnaissance on a side street in town. The grim faced cavalier sits astride his horse in a relaxed pose, cavalry saber dangling at his side. His trusty steed is bored, no doubt enjoying the brief respite from action. All too soon, "Boots and Saddles" will sound again, signaling the call to arms.

16" X 20"

The summer of 1862 was a troubled time for the Federal armies. Confederate General Robert E. Lee had defeated them repeatedly and was now invading Maryland. A twist of fate, however, gave the Federals Lee's plans, wrapped around three cigars which were found in a field at Frederick, Maryland. Union forces converged on Lee and now the showdown was at hand. September 17, 1862 would be the bloodiest single day of the American Civil War.

At 5:45 a.m. on September 17, Major General Joseph Hooker's 1st Corps marched out of the north woods south into Miller's Cornfield to attack the Confederate forces commanded by Lt. Gen. Thomas J. "Stonewall" Jackson. Hooker's Corps, some 8500 strong, was attacking Jackson's Confederates of nearly equal strength. Confederate artillery, situated on nearby Nicodemus Hill, was positioned so as to rake any forces advancing from the North Woods.

By 6:30 a.m. the men of the Iron Brigade crossed a wooden fence, passed over some open ground and entered the corn. Here, Major Rufus Dawes of the 6th Wisconsin ordered his men to lie down, as a hail of musket fire and artillery began to rain upon the field. When the men rose and advanced through the field, they began to take losses and bent down as if marching through a rainstorm. Casualties mounted as artillery case shot and shell exploded over the advancing blue line. One shell killed or wounded thirteen men. Soon the Federals came to the edge of the field, to open ground facing the Hagerstown Turnpike. Suddenly, a line of Confeder-

ates arose from their prone position behind a rail fence on the far side of the road and let loose a devastating volley which was answered simultaneously by Dawes' men. "Men I cannot say fell; they were knocked out of the ranks by the dozens," he would write, " But we jumped over the fence and pushed on, loading, firing, and shouting as we advanced."

The fighting became general and increased in ferocity as reinforcements from either side joined the fray. Brigadier General Abram Duryea's Brigade lost more than 300 men as it traversed the cornfield. The Confederates also took casualties as Federal artillery was sent forward into the fight. The firing was point blank and the advantage shifted back and forth. The cornfield changed hands as many as six times during the fray, before a final Confederate charge was shattered. According to one Texas soldier, "it seemed impossible for a rat to live in such a place. The dead and dying were in every direction." Forced to retreat, the rebel soldiers abandoned control of the cornfield to the Federals, "We could go no further," a Texan remembered, "They were too strong for us, cutting us down almost like grain before a cradle." General Hooker, who was himself wounded early in the attack, recalled that "every stalk of corn in the northern and greater part of the field was cut as closely as could have been done with a knife, and the slain lay in rows precisely as they had stood in the ranks a few moments before. It was never my fortune to witness a more bloody, dismal battlefield." Fighting in the cornfield had ended, but the battle of Antietam had just started.

It is symbolic of the ferocity of the fighting here that the words, 'the cornfield" evoke immediately the bloody action fought at Antietam in David R. Miller's cornfield. In a four years' long war fought primarily in farm country, one thirty acre cornfield, Miller's, earned immortality. Antietam has "the cornfield," as if there was no other. This is true only because of the efforts of the men who fought there, marching into an inferno of shot and shell that defies the imagination. Keith Rocco has captured that spirit in his painting. "Through the Cornfield" is perhaps Rocco's signature piece of Civil War artwork. The classic style of Howard Pyle and Andrew Wyeth mixes with the action to create a dreamlike quality. The 6th Wisconsin, of the Iron Brigade, commanded by Major Rufus Dawes charges forward, bent double as if in a rainstorm, into the fight.

THROUGH THE CORNFIELD

DECISION AT THE CROSSROADS

The small hamlet, Corinth, Mississippi was one of the most strategically important towns in the western Confederacy. The junction of the Memphis & Charleston and Mobile & Ohio Railroads made Corinth a vital transportation and supply center for the Confederacy. According to one Confederate general, "If defeated here [Corinth] we lose the Mississippi Valley and probably our cause."

Major General Henry W. Halleck, commanding three Union armies which had gathered at Pittsburg Landing after the Battle of Shiloh, was determined to capture Corinth. He slowly led his 120,000 man force towards the vital rail junction, determined to make no mistakes.

Opposing Halleck, and defending Corinth, was the defeated army from Shiloh under Lieutenant General Pierre G.T. Beauregard. Fortunately for the Confederates, Halleck was determined to lay siege to Corinth without bringing on a general engagement. Halleck took a month to progress the thirty odd miles from Pittsburg Landing to Corinth. When he was finally in position and ready to attack, Beauregard simply abandoned the town, leaving the Federals in command of the railroad junction but cheating them of the larger prize, the only organized Confederate army in the area.

Now, of course the situation was reversed, and it was the Federals who were required to defend Corinth. But the mighty army group was splintered and sent off on various other tasks, including garrison duty. General U.S. Grant was now in overall command in the theater. Only a force of 25,000 under the immediate command of General Rosecrans was left to hold the vitally important town which had been strengthened with a network of earthen fortifications.

As summer of 1862 waned into autumn, the Confederates mounted a determined effort to retake lost ground. Confederate Generals Earl Van Dorn and Sterling Price moved into northwest Mississippi early in October with a view to re-capturing Corinth and preventing Grant from reinforcing other Union armies invading Kentucky and Maryland. A sharp fight at Iuka in September blunted some of the Confederate threat by forcing Price to retreat, but directed the focus toward Corinth. Now the united forces of Price and Van Dorn moved against Rosecrans.

On October 3rd the Confederates launched a savage attack upon Corinth. Two brigades of rebels, from Dabney Maury's division, consisting of Arkansans, Missourians and Mississippians, pierced the Union lines northwest of town.

On October 4th, the battle resumed, with the attacking Confederates capturing Battery Powell and storming Battery Robinett. Despite the murderous effect of Union artillery fire, the Confederates swarmed into town to seize the rail junction. Advancing down Polk, Jackson and Fillmore streets the rebels drove the Yankees before them, and made their way into the heart of the town, fighting their way through the streets until they gained a foothold at the main prize, the vital rail junction. The fighting swirled around the crossroads and the landmark Tishimingo Hotel which faced the Memphis &Charleston Railroad. Colonel John V. DuBois' Illinois brigade, firing from behind a hasty barricade of boxes and barrels, furiously resisted the Confederate onslaught, killing their commander, Colonel William H. Moore and mowing down the rebels, whose lines "melted under their fire like snow in thaw." The Confederates resisted the counterattack but finally succumbed to the fierce resistance and timely Union reinforcements. The Federals, "with a shout that was heard through our whole lines," drove the Confederates from town, slamming the door on the missed opportunity for the Confederates. The crisis had passed.

The painting depicts the vicious fighting which occurred right at the crossroads of the two key railroads. Based on an historic photo, the noted Tishimingo Hotel, which was burned in January 1865 by retreating Confederates, stands at the left of the work, with the railway station directly across from it. Illinois troops are firing from behind barricades in the right foreground and charging across the railroad to blunt the Confederate attack. The distinctive flag carried by the Confederates at center in front of the rail depot is the Van Dorn flag, which was carried by the Army of the trans-Mississippi. It was favored by troops from Arkansas, Missouri, Texas and Mississippi. A white crescent moon and thirteen stars in five diagonal rows rest on a red field. Colonel Moore, mounted at center, is depicted moments before his death.

DECISION AT THE CROSSROADS

December 11, 1862 was a very long day for the Army of the Potomac, commanded by Major General Ambrose E. Burnside. The general planned to cross his army over the Rappahannock River on pontoon bridges and then assault the Confederate Army of Northern Virginia, which was in position on the heights behind the city of Fredericksburg, Virginia. Nothing had gone according to plan, however. Despite an early start that morning by the army's engineers, the Federal crossing had been stymied by the determined resistance of a brigade of Confederate soldiers posted in the town to thwart and delay the crossing. The engineers were driven from their work no less than nine times as they tried to complete the bridges. Burnside reacted to the delay with force. He ordered a bombardment of the town and the riverbank where the rebel sharpshooters were posted. Despite the destructive rain of shot and shell that destroyed many colonial era homes and businesses and ignited dozens of fires, the pesky defenders maintained their positions. It was not until several regiments of infantry conducted an amphibious assault, crossing in pontoons and establishing a bridgehead on the riverbank that Burnside was able to make any progress with his battle plans.

However once the bridgehead was established the Northern army could not cross in force until the town was secured. The Confederate commander in charge of defending the town was Colonel John Fiser. For most of the day, it was Fiser's direction of the detachment from William Barksdale's brigade that had stymied the efforts of the Federal engineers. Now that a lodgment at the edge of town had been made, it was Fiser's task to stage a defense, with a view towards making a withdrawal.

Fiser's men, detachments from the 13th and 17th Mississippi, abandoned their positions along the riverbank and fell back to a secondary line. Making good use of materials at hand, a network of barricades had been prepared for just such a contingency. The spaces between houses and alleyways were blocked with dirt-filled boxes, barrels, boards and other materials. Additionally, soldiers took positions in loop-holed homes, cellars and storehouses along the streets that run from the river into town, creating a deadly gantlet for the attackers as they battled their way into the town.

The Union attack was led by Colonel Norman J. Hall's brigade, which was crammed into the small area between the Rappahannock River and Sophia Street where the first Federal troops to cross the river were staging. The 7th Michigan and 19th Massachusetts Infantry regiments were ordered to advance up parallel streets and take out resistance in the town, clearing the way for the Federal advance. What followed was perhaps the first occurrence of urban street fighting in the Civil War. The attackers channeled their way up the streets in a column of companies. The advance was met by withering volleys that swept away the heads of the attacking columns, resulting in what one Confederate called, "a dreadful slaughter." Whole platoons were knocked out of line. Part of the 19th Massachusetts Infantry took shelter in a blind alley, away from the deadly volleys of the defenders. Despite heavy losses, Hall's men bullied their way forward. The fiercest fighting occurred with the advance of the 20th Massachusetts. Now the Federals fought house to house, yard to yard and drove out the defenders, often engaging in fierce hand-to-hand combat as they inched their way to a toehold along Caroline Street. Finally, when Fiser saw that his line had been irreparably penetrated, he ordered his men to fall back and abandon the town. The defenders had done their job, both buying Robert E. Lee an entire day to perfect his lines, and disrupting the timetable of attack for Burnside. The town of Fredericksburg was in Yankee possession after the unexpectedly difficult day of fighting. But the worst was yet to come.

Keith Rocco captures the spirit of this fighting in all of its intensity, putting the viewer right in the middle of the action from the viewpoint of the Confederate defenders.

The painting captures the fluidity of the tactical situation. Fiser's Mississippians run from one position to another to meet the Federal thrust. Soldiers are firing around the corner of the Lewis Store, which still stands on the corner of Lewis and Caroline Streets. Constructed in 1749, it is the oldest building in Fredericksburg, and claims George Washington as a customer. On the left, soldiers are seen crouching and firing from behind a fence. Smoke from fires set during the artillery bombardment wafts over the defenders.

Unlike many other states, New Hampshire did not have a formally organized militia at the outset of the Civil War. There were several volunteer militia companies in existence, but none of them were suitably manned or equipped for the demanding service of the war. The state was required to provide one regiment in response to President Lincoln's call for 75,000 volunteers to put down the rebellion, and quickly complied. By fall of 1861 more regiments were required. One of these was the 5th New Hampshire.

The 5th New Hampshire was organized at Concord, New Hampshire in August 1861 under the authority of Governor Nathaniel S. Berry. Colonel Edward Cross, of Lancaster, was given command of the new regiment, which was soon sent to Washington, D.C. to become part of the main Union army. Colonel Cross, by trade a newspaperman, is largely credited with shaping and defining the 5th New Hampshire. Cross was not without military experience, having fought Indians in Arizona and Mexico. His rigid discipline and insistence on drill and other training made this volunteer regiment a crack outfit, the equal of many regular army regiments. Cross organized a school for his junior and non-commissioned officers to make them proficient in drill and tactics, teaching them that "implicit obedience to orders was one of the cardinal virtues in a soldier."

Cross was determined to outfit his men with the best uniforms and equipment available. Instead of the usual militia gray, which Cross regarded as being of inferior quality, he commandeered from Concord new regulation uniforms. Thus, his men were outfitted with "brogans, light-blue trousers and overcoat with cape, and dark-blue blouse and frock coat, and to cap us a helmet-like structure of dark gray or blue-mixed waterproof cloth, with a visor before and behind…This was a New Hampshire cap."

The regiment has the distinction of having sustained the greatest losses in battle of any regiment in the Union Army during the Civil War. It fought during the Seven Days' Battles around Richmond, and in the Bloody Lane at Antietam where it lost 127 men killed and wounded. Writing about Antietam, Colonel Cross recalled, "My men fought nobly, gloriously…Not a man but the wounded and dead fell out." Cross was struck five times at Antietam. At Fredericksburg, in December 1862, the regiment again suffered severely when 249 men and nineteen officers, alongside the Irish Brigade, went into action against the stone wall at the base of Marye's Heights. During the assault, every officer in the regiment was killed or wounded, including Cross who was wounded twice. Only seventy men were present for duty the next day, the rest had fallen. It was here at Fredericksburg that the regiment earned its moniker, "The Fighting Fifth." The 5th was present at Chancellorsville but was held in reserve. At Gettysburg, the 5th New Hampshire went into action in the Wheatfield on July 2, 1862. Here, they lost 86 men out of 177 who went into action. Among the slain was Colonel Cross who had been raised to brigade command. Afterwards the regiment was sent home to rest and recruit new members. It returned to the field for the 1864 campaigns, fighting in the Wilderness, Spotsylvania, Cold Harbor and Petersburg. The reputation of the 5th New Hampshire was well earned. No less a personage than Major General Winfield Scott Hancock wrote, "The conduct of this regiment has been heroic: in the most important battles it has been highly distinguished."

In Keith Rocco's painting, a junior officer is shown wearing the field uniform of the 5th New Hampshire as they appeared in late 1862, about the time of the Battle of Fredericksburg. He is wearing a custom made dark overcoat with cape and a knit scarf, perhaps a gift from home or something made by the women of his hometown and shipped off to the regiment. The officer wears the red officer's kepi issued to New Hampshire's regiments early in the war, and carries an imported staff officer's sword. Like most officers, he was free to purchase tailor made uniforms and customized equipment.

PRIVATE COLLECTION   5TH NEW HAMPSHIRE INFANTRY OFFICER   12" X 9"

14TH BROOKLYN

One of the more colorful and memorable units in the Civil War was the 14th Brooklyn, an infantry regiment that was raised and outfitted in 1861. The regiment had its origins as a volunteer militia unit originally organized on July 5, 1847 in the Brooklyn Heights District. In it's ranks were some of the who's who of the city. Though the antebellum unit served primarily as a ceremonial troop, it took a fastidious pride in its appearance and drill. The official designation of the regiment was the 84th New York Infantry, but the unit was allowed to maintain its identity as the 14th Brooklyn, by special order of Major General Irvin McDowell as a reward for its gallant service.

The uniform of the 14th was a chasseur style outfit modeled on the French fashion for light infantry regiments. A skirted blue chasseur jacket sporting a double row of fourteen brass buttons was complemented by dark red wool trousers and a red waistcoat with fourteen brass buttons, its sleeves trimmed with red chevrons. White gaiters with seven buttons were worn over the shoes and the outfit was topped off with a navy blue and red forage cap, or kepi, ornamented with the brass numerals "14" and company letter. For dress parade, white gauntlets and paper collars were worn. The regiment was one of the few to maintain its showy uniform for the duration of its service. On the march or in battle, their flamboyant display never failed to attract attention. One Confederate officer, viewing them on the march, opined, "their appearance was indeed magnificent."

The "Red Legged Devils" earned their nickname at the First Battle of Bull Run, where they charged the slopes of Henry House Hill four times. Despite being repulsed

with heavy losses, their relentless aggression caught the attention of both the Union and Confederate armies. The nickname was bestowed upon them by no less a personage than Stonewall Jackson who cautioned his Virginians "Hold on Boys! Here come those red legged devils again." The reputation was one they never failed to live up to in the battles that followed, including Gaines Mill, Second Bull Run, Antietam, Fredericksburg and Chancellorsville. The regiment was famous enough that President Lincoln often inquired about it and designated it as his escort whenever he visited the army.

On the morning of July 1, 1863, Lysander Cutler's Brigade was the vanguard of the 1st Corps as it neared Gettysburg. Led by Colonel Edward B. Fowler, the 14th Brooklyn trailed the second brigade as it trudged along the Emmitsburg Road. The roar of artillery interspersed with small arms fire told that there would be "serious work ahead," en route to McPherson's Woods, where Federal cavalry had been engaged with Confederate infantry. As the regiment went into line along the Emmitsburg Road, it began to take heavy fire. During the opening stages of their involvement in the battle, General John Reynolds, commander of the I Corps, was killed. Men of the 14th Brooklyn carried him from the field. The battle for the woods raged in their front when they began taking additional fire from the flank and rear.

The regiment was ordered to drop its packs and double quick march into action. Confederate General J.R. Davis' Mississippi brigade was advancing through a railroad cut and firing upon Cutler's men. The 14th Brooklyn, joining with the 6th Wisconsin and 95th New York regiments, changed front and stormed the railroad cut, capturing hundreds of Confederates of Davis' brigade of Mississippians, who "fought with the ferocity of wildcats." Later, the 14th fought with distinction at Culp's Hill, on July 2nd and 3rd, and were credited with saving the Union position there. The 14th Brooklyn is the only regiment to have three markers on Gettysburg Battlefield; one at McPherson's Woods, another at the railroad cut and the third atop Culp's Hill.

The 14th Brooklyn continued to fight and sustain its reputation through the spring of 1864, fighting at the Wilderness and Spotsylvania Court House. At the end of May, 1864, the veterans of the 14th Brooklyn returned to New York. After receiving a fitting heroes' welcome, the veterans formed up to muster out and return home. Their service had ended, but their legacy was immortal.

In the painting, members of the 14th Brooklyn New York State Militia are going into action, crouching over to avoid incoming fire as they load and fire their muskets just as they are about to advance. They are clad in their trademark chasseur uniform, which is begrimed by the hard march over muddy roads they made to reach Gettysburg.

14TH BROOKLYN

"To be a Confederate soldier meant for the Marylander, in addition to hardship and danger, exile from home and kindred," wrote Randolph McKim, of the 2nd Maryland Infantry, C.S.A.

One of the goals of Robert E. Lee's invasion of Maryland in September 1862 was to recruit fresh volunteers into his dwindled ranks. The popular belief at the time, shared by the Army of Tennessee's commander Braxton Bragg, was that thousands of volunteers were waiting to join the ranks of the Confederacy in Maryland and Kentucky. All that was lacking was a strong Confederate presence to afford them the opportunity. As time would tell, those ideas were more wishful thinking than reality and only a handful of men joined the Confederate armies.

The 2nd Maryland Infantry was the only regiment from that state to serve in the Army of Northern Virginia. The 2nd Maryland was organized in Fall, 1862 in Winchester, Virginia. The regiment was recruited from men of the disbanding 1st Maryland which had enlisted for only one year and the recruits who were gathered during the Antietam Campaign. The men of the regiment were "gentlemen and had the pride necessary for making good soldiers," according to one officer. Colonel James R. Herbert commanded the newly organized regiment which joined the Army of Northern Virginia. The newly formed regiment served in the Shenandoah until the beginning of the Gettysburg Campaign, skirmishing with the enemy at Winchester, and operating against railroads.

The 2nd Maryland fought with distinction at Gettysburg. As they marched from the valley into Maryland, it was difficult to hold back tears at thoughts of the homes they could not return to. The 2nd Maryland was assigned to Brigadier General George H. Steuart's brigade. Following a long weary trek the men arrived at Gettysburg on the evening of July 1st, marching past the carnage of the first days' battle and pausing to rest in the streets of town before going into line along the Hanover Pike.

On the evening of July 2nd, at Culp's Hill they participated in Steuart's attack. The Confederates had spent a trying day awaiting the sounds of attacks on other parts of the field. They finally went into action late in the day, attacking Union forces on Culp's Hill, where they overran the Union fortifications. They succeeded in capturing part of the line, but lost more than a hundred men in the bloody fighting, including Colonel Herbert who was struck three times. On the following day, the 2nd again attacked. Steuart's brigade formed at right angles to the entrenchments they had taken the previous night and charged the Federal position, making a direct frontal assault. The advance led them into an open field, two hundred yards from the Union line. The Federal position was heavily manned and the fire they brought to bear on the Marylanders was devastating. The 2nd Maryland was decimated, losing 189 men, almost half of those engaged. In two days' fighting they sustained more than 300 casualties.

The 2nd Maryland remained with the Army of Northern Virginia for the duration of the war, fighting in every campaign and battle including the Wilderness, Spotsylvania, Cold Harbor and the siege of Petersburg. By spring 1865 only a handful of the regiment remained. These surrendered with the rest of Lee's army at Appomattox Court House.

Like their more famous Kentucky counterparts, the Marylanders fought through the war knowing they were orphans. While they fought, the enemy occupied their home state. These Marylanders had little chance or hope of returning to the homes they had left. "Oh the loneliness of the Maryland soldier…" wrote McKim, "Oh! The unutterable longing then for the faces of those whom he had left behind!"

Our Marylander is dressed in their typical uniform, waist length gray shell jacket and trousers, forage cap and knapsack. Maryland's soldiers were atypically well dressed compared to other Confederates for most of the war. He sports the "Maryland Cross" on his breast. Representative of the Flowering cross of Avalon, it is part of the heraldry of Maryland and is emblazoned on the state flag.

PRIVATE COLLECTION   2ND MARYLAND   16" X 12"

Little Round Top is the name given to a hill situated one of the most widely visited spots on any Civil War battlefield. The rocky knoll to the west of Gettysburg anchored the left of the Union line along Cemetery Ridge and overlooks the area of some of the fiercest fighting, including the Wheatfield and Devil's Den. Called Little Round Top because it is adjacent to a similar but larger wooded knoll, Big Round Top, the hill gained immortality because of what happened, and what didn't happen, on its slopes on the late afternoon of July 2, 1863.

As a Confederate attack on the left flank crashed down upon the Union III Corps, which had taken an advanced position overlooking the Emmitsburg Road, Brigadier General Gouverneur K. Warren observed that Little Round Top was held by nothing more than a Signal Corps detachment. The general hurriedly diverted Colonel Strong Vincent's brigade of infantry to the summit, which he correctly assessed as the key to the Union position. Vincent's V Corps brigade had been ordered to reinforce Sickles. Warren acted just in time as Little Round Top was the objective of the Confederate attack.

The 20th Maine Infantry was posted at the extreme left flank of the Union line and ordered to hold the position at all hazards. Colonel Joshua Lawrence Chamberlain, a divinity professor from Bowdoin College in Brunswick, Maine, commanded the 20th Maine. Chamberlain was to become the unlikely "savior" of the Union army.

As the bluecoats advanced up the slopes of the hill they began taking Confederate artillery fire. Dodging the exploding shells and shattered tree branches, 386 men and their officers from Maine clambered up the slopes and went into line amid the boulders that jutted out from the hill, piling up rocks to make breastworks. "All but the drummer boys and hospital attendants" were poised to defend the position. Chamberlain arranged his men into line and refused the flank by adjusting several companies to form a right angle with the main line. Chamberlain completed his

dispositions just as Confederate Colonel William C. Oates led his 15th Alabama up the slopes to attack.

Chamberlain's men opened fire as the Confederates approached within fifty yards of their position. The devastating volley, "the most destructive fire I ever saw," according to Oates, staggered the Alabamians, who fell back to regroup. In the next two hours, Oates and his men made five desperate attacks, each time falling just short of breaking Chamberlain's line, which they briefly pierced, before being driven back. Fatigue from long marching and hard fighting, coupled with lack of water began to take its toll. On the Federal side, Chamberlain's men were running out of ammunition and hastened to gather rounds from the cartridge boxes of the dead and wounded lying around.

As the Confederates prepared to make another assault, Chamberlain made a rash decision. Knowing that his ammunition was short and that the stamina of his men was waning, he opted to counter-attack. The colonel rose up, positioning himself near the colors, uttering the command, "Fix Bayonets!" According to Chamberlain, that word was enough. "It ran like fire along the line…and rose into a shout." Chamberlain's men charged down the slope while wheeling to the right. The impact of the charge took all of the momentum out of the Confederate attack. Chamberlain's 200 survivors drove Oates' Alabamians down the slopes of Little Round Top, capturing scores of them. The ferocity of the attack was decisive. The 20th Maine drove the Confederates from the slopes of Little Round Top, dispersing the remainder who fled to shelter in a disorganized body. The crisis for possession of Little Round Top had passed. The union flank was secured. The Confederates would have to try again. Another day. Another location.

Keith Rocco's painting captures the dramatic moment as the command to fix bayonets is given. Standing behind one of the granite boulders, Chamberlain is unsheathing his sword, steeling himself for the charge. Men, some of them wounded, are preparing to advance as they attach their bayonets. The late afternoon sun is breaching the trees overhead, glorious rays of sunlight shimmering through the branches. The contrast of brilliant light and the grim determination in the posture of the men is stark. The intensity of the struggle is given testimony by the haggard expressions in the faces and the eyes of the soldiers, in the wounded lying against a tree further up the slope, and in the focus of the men to the left, still firing at an unseen foe.

Fix Bayonets

14" X 21"

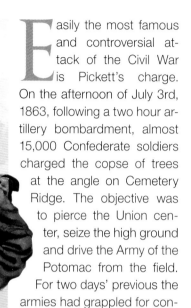

Easily the most famous and controversial attack of the Civil War is Pickett's charge. On the afternoon of July 3rd, 1863, following a two hour artillery bombardment, almost 15,000 Confederate soldiers charged the copse of trees at the angle on Cemetery Ridge. The objective was to pierce the Union center, seize the high ground and drive the Army of the Potomac from the field. For two days' previous the armies had grappled for control of the heights surrounding the crossroads town. Confederate General Robert E. Lee was making a final, determined effort to win the day.

The Confederates making the charge were from the divisions of George Pickett, James Pettigrew, and William D. Pender. Nine brigades of Confederates advanced on the Union lines, covering a front of about a mile. The charge was made over 1400 yards of mostly open ground, making the attackers vulnerable every step of the way to Union artillery, and as they neared the objective, deadly musketry and canister fire.

Union Colonel Frank Haskell was an eyewitness to the charge and described it: "Every eye could see the enemy's legions, an overwhelming resistless tide of an ocean of armed men sweeping upon us! Regiment after regiment and brigade after brigade move from the woods and rapidly take their places in the line forming the assault. Pickett's proud division with some additional troops hold their right. The first line at short intervals is followed by a second, and that a third succeeds; and columns between support the lines…" It was a grand spectacle one could not help but admire. Major General Winfield Scott Hancock, commanding the Union II Corps recalled, "Their lines were formed with a precision and steadiness that extorted the admiration of the witnesses of that memorable scene."

Despite their admiration of the spectacle, the Union defenders did their utmost to destroy it. The Federals on Cemetery Ridge were aware of their duty and they ex-

ecuted it with great effect. Shot and shell from artillery, combined with sustained volleys of musketry made the Confederates pay dearly for every forward step.

Captain Henry T. Owen, of the 18th Virginia of Garnett's Brigade recalled that "The destruction of life in the ranks of that advancing host was fearful beyond precedent, officers going down by dozens and the men by scores and fifties." Despite the horrific losses the Confederates advanced relentlessly, taking advantage of momentary cover from swells in the ground to dress their lines, consolidating their front to one-half mile. Steadily, unbelievably, they advanced into the maelstrom of death and neared the Union lines, making a final, desperate push for the Ridge and the guns upon it.

Confederate Brigadier General Richard B. Garnett had defied orders to lead his brigade on horseback, making him an obvious and conspicuous target. The general was recovering from an injury and need not have made the assault. Garnett and his brigade neared to within 200 yards of the stone wall when the magnitude of the fire hitting them increased in intensity. Garnett tried to steady what was left of his brigade for the final push into the very faces of the Union defenders. Running, oblivious now to commands to dress the lines, the attackers pushed on. A devastating volley dropped many of them. Garnett's riderless horse, bleeding at the shoulder, was observed fleeing the field. The gallant general's body was never identified.

Briefly, all too briefly, the Confederate juggernaut broke the Union line. But there were too few of them to exploit the break. Met by a furious counterattack, many surrendered rather than retrace their steps across the killing fields. The attack failed with a loss of greater than fifty per cent. Garnett's brigade lost 941 men and officers out of the 1,427 who made the charge. As he viewed the shattered remnants of the attacking force, Robert E. Lee rode out to meet them. "It is all my fault," he assured them.

"Hell for Glory" is the title of Keith Rocco's depiction of Garnett's brigade during the final moments of Pickett's Charge. The general is seen, dressed in his resplendent new uniform, waving his hat as he urges his men on in the last leg of the charge. In seconds he will fall, to be seen no more. The banner of the 18th Virginia waves defiantly as it advances, carried by Lt. Col. Henry A. Carrington. The grim determination is clearly seen in the faces of the attackers as they advance, regardless of the cost.

PICKETT'S CHARGE

The 54th Massachusetts was a volunteer regiment of black soldiers, raised and outfitted in Boston, in 1863. Although it was not the first regiment of Colored Troops to serve in the Union armies, it would be the first black regiment raised in the North. After the enactment of the Emancipation Proclamation in January, 1863, Massachusetts Governor Andrew Curtin received authorization to raise regiments that could include persons of African descent. Curtin, backed by Frederick Douglass, the famous orator, abolitionist and former slave, recruited the regiment. Two of Douglass' sons were among the first recruits in the regiment, which filled its ranks with free men. The colonel of the regiment, Robert Gould Shaw, was from one of the most prominent Boston families. The 54th Massachusetts Infantry was a showcase regiment by design. After completing its training and marching through the streets of Boston to great fanfare, the regiment was shipped to the Department of the South.

In speaking of the use of black soldiers, Abraham Lincoln wrote, "The colored population is the great available and yet unavailed of, force for restoring the Union. The bare sight of fifty thousand armed, and drilled black soldiers on the banks of the Mississippi, would end the rebellion at once."

At first the regiment was assigned to manual labor and fatigue duties, but it also participated in raids, including burning the town of Darien. In a skirmish on July 16th, 1863 the 54th was instrumental in blunting a Confederate attack. On July 18, 1863, the 54th, led by its dashing young commander, Lt. Colonel Robert Gould Shaw charged into glory. Fort Wagner was an earthen work fortification situated on the point of Morris Island in Charleston Harbor. Capture of the fort would enable Union forces to threaten the city of Charleston.

The attackers had to run a hellish half mile gantlet across a narrow strip of beach, a sixty yard front that was expertly ranged by the Confederate artillerists in the fort. General Seymour Strong's brigade led the attack. Strong's brigade was made up of the 54th Massachusetts, 6th Connecticut, 48th New York, 3rd New Hampshire, 76th Pennsylvania and 9th Maine. At dusk the attackers advanced in a column of regiments due to the narrow approach to the fort, which meant the attacking formation would be tightly compacted. As a consequence, casualties would be high. Strong's brigade was followed by the brigades of Putnam and Stevenson. As a prelude to the assault Union artillery, augmented from fire by ironclad gunboats in the harbor and land batteries on Morris Island, shelled the fort. As the brigade marched slowly to the attack, it was immediately met by a barrage of shot and shell. Artillery in Fort Wagner, supported by the guns of Fort Sumter and the batteries on Cummings Point rained death on the attackers.

Braving this horrendous fire and losing men with every step, some of the attackers managed to charge through the ditches, reach the ramparts of the fort and engage the defenders in hand to hand combat. For nearly an hour the furious assault continued, until every officer in the lead regiments were killed or wounded. Colonel Shaw was dead, lying among the bravest of his men on the ramparts of the fort. Despite driving the Confederate gunners away at bayonet point, the attack stalled. The survivors were forced to retrace their steps across the killing fields. A second wave of attackers met a similar fate. Fort Wagner was not to be taken.

The attack on Fort Wagner was monumental in its implications. Although this would not be the first instance of African-American soldiers fighting in the war, it would be the most compelling to that time. The death of Shaw and his burial with his men, meant by the Confederates as an insult, was instead viewed as an honor. The fighting prowess of black soldiers was proven beyond a doubt. The 54th Massachusetts lost 256 officers and men in the assault.

The painting depicts the doomed assault on Fort Wagner. From the perspective of the men making the assault the grim fate awaiting those on the parapet is clear to see. The staggering human price of the attack is clearly stated as men stumble and fall and squirm on the earthworks. Keith Rocco's painting was commissioned especially for the Abraham Lincoln Museum in Springfield, Illinois.

Fort Wagner

36" X 33"

MOSBY'S RANGERS

Among the more colorful units raised during the war were the informal cavalry, or partisan rangers. The most famous unit of these was raised and commanded by Col. John Singleton Mosby who came to renown as the Gray Ghost. Originally an enlistee in the 1st Virginia Cavalry, Mosby attracted the attention of Confederate Cavalry commander James E.B. (Jeb) Stuart, and took a staff position under him. Mosby's skills at reconnaissance and raiding paved the way for him to raise and exercise an independent command group of partisan rangers, who gained far-reaching importance and fame. Loudon County, in northwestern Virginia, came to be known as Mosby's Confederacy.

Among Mosby's more renowned feats was the capture of Brigadier General Edwin H. Stoughton on March 9, 1863. On that rainy evening, Mosby and thirty-nine of his men raided into Fairfax Courthouse, Virginia with a view towards capturing Sir Percy Wyndham who had made disparaging remarks about Mosby. Learning that Wyndham was not present, but that Brigadier General Edwin Stoughton was, Mosby entered the room where the general was asleep. Mosby roused Stoughton with a spank on the rump and asked if he had ever heard of Mosby. When the groggy general asked if Mosby had been captured, Mosby identified himself and informed Stoughton that it was he who was captured. In addition to the general, the band made off with thirty Federal soldiers and fifty-eight horses, catapulting Mosby into celebrity. When President Lincoln learned of the escapade he expressed more concern over the loss of the horses than of Stoughton, stating that he could make brigadier generals, but he couldn't make horses.

On January 9-10, 1864 while raiding in the upper Shenandoah Valley, at Loudon Heights in the vicinity of Harper's Ferry, Mosby learned from Captain Benjamin Franklin "Frank" Stringfellow, another of J.E.B. Stuart's scouts, Federal cavalry under Colonel Henry A. Cole were encamped nearby. Cole's force of Maryland cavalry had been dogging Mosby deep in his territory and had actually been defeated in a sharp fight on January 1st. Now, thanks to Stringfellow's scouting efforts, the Federal camp had been discovered. Stringfellow reported that Cole's Battalion was doing picket duty near Harper's Ferry, but that they were only watching one road. Stringfellow believed that he could lead Mosby into the camp and capture everyone without firing a shot. Mosby and Stringfellow decided upon a night attack to take Cole completely by surprise. Mosby

took a force of one hundred men and approached Cole's camp. The plan, according to Mosby, was to send Stringfellow ahead with ten men to capture Cole and his staff from the house they were using, then to charge into the camp, taking everybody by surprise.

But, as often happened in a night action, confusion reigned. Mosby approached along a narrow path, getting within two hundred yards of the Federal camp without being detected. The camp was in a state of quietude; not a single sentry was posted or awake. Thinking everything was going as expected, he sent Stringfellow in. According to Mosby, "All my plans were on the eve of consummation, when suddenly the party sent with Stringfellow came dashing over the hill, toward the camp yelling and shooting. They had made no attempt to secure Cole. Mistaking them for the enemy, I ordered my men to charge." Chaos ensued. The Federals, alerted by Stringfellow's shooting, met Mosby's headlong charge into their midst with a volley of fire from their carbines. Instead of springing a trap, Mosby had ridden into one. Knowing the Federals were likely to get reinforcements, he had no choice but retreat, bringing out six prisoners and about sixty horses. But the cost of this miserly success was high: four killed, seven wounded (four mortally) and one captured.

This night raid upon Cole's camp is known as the Battle of Loudon Heights and is typical of the nature of Mosby's hit and run tactics. His small irregular band of partisan rangers disrupted Federal supply lines and communications and kept an inordinate number of Federal cavalry and infantry busy, preventing their use elsewhere. He became one of the most legendary figures of the war. Frank Stringfellow also had a reputation as a raider and scout and at one point was regarded as the "most dangerous man in the Confederacy," with a bounty of $10,000 offered for his capture.

The painting depicts Mosby seated right of center in a red cape and Stringfellow, at center, leaning over to discuss the plans in front of St. Paul's Episcopal Church in Haymarket. A number of mounted rangers are huddled about in the cold, waiting for the word to advance.

MOSBY'S RANGERS

The opening stages of the Wilderness Campaign in May 1864 heralded a change in the nature of the Civil War. With the ascension of Lieutenant General Ulysses S. Grant to overall command of the Union armies, the new strategy would be to engage the Confederate armies and fight them simultaneously, preventing them from reinforcing each other. Grim arithmetic, based on superior Union manpower, promised a Union victory so long as the Confederates were pinned down. Grant, accompanying the Army of the Potomac, commanded by Major General George Gordon Meade would be facing General Robert E. Lee and the Army of Northern Virginia for the first time. Grant was determined to strike hard and fast, but the outnumbered Confederates struck first.

Major General Gouverneur K. Warren's V Corps led the Union advance into the Wilderness the morning of May 5, 1864. As Warren's strung out corps made its way through the thickets along the narrow road, they encountered a line of Confederates. Warren reported the strong enemy and began deploying his men. Convinced that this enemy force was only an advance guard, Grant and Meade ordered Warren to attack without regard to his dispositions. Warren ordered the assault before he could concentrate his corps and protect his flanks. The unhappy duty fell to Major General Charles Griffin, commanding the first division. His objective was the line of Confederates posted in the woods across the open ground at Saunders Field, a large oval-shaped unused cornfield, measuring approximately 500 yards by 400 yards. Situated along the Orange Turnpike it was one of the few open spaces in the Wilderness. The Orange Turnpike cut through the field which sloped upwards east to west. The only shelter in the field was the stubble of last year's cornstalks and a gully which cut across the field.

Griffin was not at all happy with the order or with the disposition of his men. Warren was actually in agreement with Griffin, but had direct orders to attack without regard to his dispositions. Despite his own convictions, he directed the assault to proceed as ordered.

Brigadier General Romeyn B. Ayres' brigade was selected to spearhead the attack. Ayres' men deployed in two lines to open the attack. The 140th New York, a Zouave regiment, went in first, supported by the 146th New York, also a Zouave unit. As the colorfully dressed men prepared to advance they could clearly hear the sound of axes and falling trees from the Confederates' position in dense woods at the far end of the field.

The defenders were in fact much more than an advance guard. Ayres was attacking Lieutenant General Richard S. Ewell's II Corps, 14,000 of Lee's battle hardened veterans. The Confederates across Sanders Field were under the cover of thick woods and were busily constructing field fortifications. Every moment of delay in the attack made the Confederate position that much stronger.

The 140th New York began their assault in the noon hour and advanced through the tangle of underbrush and scrub trees into the open, sunlit field. The Union line was immediately met by a long range volley from the woods. After a momentary pause to align, the attack began across the open field with a fierce cheer. This was answered by murderous volleys. Gaps appeared in the battle lines as men were knocked out in clusters, disappearing "as if the earth had swallowed them up." Despite this, the New Yorkers reached the woods and engaged in hand to hand fighting with the defenders. Taking fire from the front and unsupported flanks, the 140th was in trouble.

The 146th New York advanced to their support but they also were staggered by Confederate volleys. Corporal Norton C. Shepard wrote, "We had only smoke and evergreen to fire at, whereas we stood out in the plain sunlight, a good target for our foe." Adding to the woes of the beleaguered attackers, they began taking friendly fire from their own artillery. No one could withstand such punishment. As the 146th joined the 140th, they were taking fire from their front, flanks and rear. At the critical moment, Brigadier General John M. Jones' Virginia brigade charged from the south as two other Confederates brigades charged from the north. Ayres brigade crumbled. The survivors ran for their lives. "We were in a bag, and the bag was tied," wrote Captain Sweet, of the 146th New York.

The painting depicts the charge of the colorful 140th and 146th New York across the amber field of corn stumps and mustard grass. Confederates fire volleys from the cover of the woods on the left. The dramatic contrast of color is hauntingly beautiful, belying the hellish reality of the action. And Hell it was, for smoldering embers from musket wadding set the field ablaze, dooming the badly wounded to a horrible death.

INTO THE WILDERNESS

VICTORY OR DEATH

April 6th, 1865 was the "Black Thursday" of the Confederacy. As Robert E. Lee's Army of Northern Virginia fell back from its entrenchments at Petersburg, the Union forces pursued, sensing victory was within their grasp. Lee intended to re-supply his army and retreat into North Carolina, where conceivably he could unite his forces with those of General Joseph E. Johnston. The united armies could then turn either on Sherman, who was pursuing Johnston, or Grant, who was pursuing Lee. Either way there would be strength in numbers.

But the Federals were not about to let such a contingency develop. Lee's moves were blocked at every turn and he was shepherded away from the North Carolina line westward towards Appomattox Court House. Near Farmville, Lee's rearguard was brought to bay at Sailor's Creek. Union cavalry was continuously striking at Lee's supply wagons, forcing the column to slow down to defend itself. Late in the afternoon of this long day, the rearguard of Lee's army took a hasty defensive position along Sailor's Creek, a small meandering stream.

Confederate General Richard S. Ewell corps was assigned the thankless rear guard duties. As Federal cavalry continued to harass the Confederate flanks, Ewell deployed his men along the high ground across the river from the Federals in the vicinity of a small farmhouse. His diminished corps consisted of the divisions of Joseph B. Kershaw, George Washington Custis Lee and a battalion of marines and sailors from the Drewry's Bluff garrison. Custis Lee, son of the commanding general, was assigned to protect the Confederate left. Lee's division was sadly depleted, and contained a variety of under strength, poorly armed units, including heavy artillery units serving as infantry, one of which was the Savannah Volunteer Guards.

The Union VI Corps, commanded by Major General Horatio Wright was advancing against the Confederates, having driven them across Sailors Creek. As Wright prepared for his attack, Federal artillery bombarded the Confederate lines. Ewell had no artillery to counter fire and his men were forced to helplessly endure the bombardment.

In the ensuing attack, the Federals were initially stymied by a furious counter-attack. Refusing to surrender without a fight, the Confederates actually drove back the first wave of attackers. "I was

never more astonished," Wright confessed. Wright was not easily dissuaded however. Reforming his lines, which now overlapped both Confederate flanks, the final charge was made. The Confederate line was crushed as hand to hand combat broke out all along the front. The Union soldiers taunted the Confederates, waving white handkerchiefs in an effort to induce them to surrender.

In Lee's front, the Savannah Volunteer Guards were overrun by the 121st New York Infantry. After a severe struggle, in which the elite Guards unit lost almost two-thirds of its men, the New Yorkers emerged victorious, capturing the battle flag of the artillerymen and also bagging General Custis Lee. The Confederates realized they had no choice and many of them surrendered to this overwhelming attack. Among those captured were six generals, including Ewell and Custis Lee, and some 3,400 fighting men. Coupled with similar disasters nearby, at Marshall's Crossroads, the southerners realized that the last days of the Confederacy were at hand. Later that evening, Robert E. Lee, seeing the demoralized fragments of his army was heard to exclaim, "My God! Has the army been dissolved?"

In the painting "Victory or Death," (a tribute to the inscription emblazoned on its battle flag), elements of the Savannah Volunteer Guards are depicted in their final moments of the fight, moments before being overrun by the 121st New York Infantry. Wearing their distinctive artillery uniforms, the remnants of this elite unit, whose origins dated to 1802, fought virtually to the last man. Only eighty-five men were present for this last attack, of which fifty-two would fall. The color guard, Sergeants Simeon Morton and Richard Millen are shown holding the flag. Soon both would be dead and the sacred flag would be in the hands of Harris S. Hawthorne of the 121st New York.

VICTORY OR DEATH

Marshall's Crossroads

When one thinks of cavalry, the image that springs to mind is of a massed charge over open ground with sabers raised to slash the enemy and hooves pounding to terrify and overwhelm an enemy. Too often, Civil War cavalry was relegated to arduous service, skirmishing, guard duty or extended raids on an enemy's communications. Very seldom was there a classical charge that stirs the imagination. Yet one such occurred on the eve of the end of the war, on April 6th at Sailor's Creek, as Union forces pressed the Confederates fleeing the trenches at Petersburg in the war's last campaign.

On that day, as the rear guard of the Confederate Army made a stand, Federal cavalry massed in the vicinity of Marshall's Crossroads, on a day that would be known as the Black Thursday of the Confederacy. Here, a short distance from Petersburg, the Federals brought the Army of Northern Virginia to bay. The Confederates were positioned in a hasty line formed along the banks of Sailor's Creek and in the fields nearby. The importance of the stand made by the Rebels this day can not be overstated; they were guarding the supplies that would enable Lee to remain in the field.

On the Federal side, here at last was an opportunity to deliver a death blow. As Union Infantry battled the Confederates at Sailor's Creek, General Wesley Merritt's three divisions of cavalry were massing for an attack against the Confederate works at Marshall's Crossroads. Brigadier General George Armstrong Custer's 3rd Division formed on the right. Brigadier General Thomas C. Devin held the center with the 1st Division. The 2nd Division, commanded by Major General George Crook took position on the left. As the charge was sounded, the ground shook under the beating hooves of thousands of horses. The impact of the charge was inevitably overwhelming.

Colonel Henry Capehart, commanding the 2nd West Virginia Cavalry led the final attack. Accompanying Capehart on this headlong, wild charge was Lieutenant Tom Custer. Capehart described the charge as follows: "one regiment in line, supported in center by two regiments in column of squadrons and one regiment supporting the right…5,000 iron hoofs were in motion." As the charged progressed over 800 yards of open ground there was a tremendous din from bugles blowing, horses thundering down upon the Confederates and the wild cheers of Union horsemen. At last the advance crashed into the Confederate line. Horses leapt over the works and down upon the defenders. Sabers and pistols were used freely, adding to the din. Those who tried to make a stand were ruthlessly slashed or shot down. In the midst of this maelstrom, Lieutenant Tom Custer, despite sustaining a wound, was able to seize a Confederate flag, his second capture in as many days, earning him a second medal of honor.

The Confederate resistance melted away in the face of the attack. Most of the defenders who did not get a chance to flee surrendered. Entire regiments gave up their arms, perhaps relieved that the war was over. In addition to 6,000 men captured, the victorious blue-clad horsemen took hundreds of Lee's supply wagons, numerous caissons and fifteen artillery pieces. Eight generals were among the captured and a large number of regimental banners, a devastating loss to the defenders but trophies of honor and distinction for the horse soldiers.

At the end of the day, when Robert E. Lee saw the tattered remnants of the day's battle and learned of the disaster to his rearguard, he cried out in despair at the apparent dissolution of his army. The end was near. The disaster at Sailor's Creek and Marshall's Crossroads was a mortal blow from which the army of Northern Virginia could not recover. In just a few days, Lee would be forced to surrender the last of his men.

The painting shows the last grand charge, as the 2nd West Virginia Cavalry thunders across the fields towards the Confederate line. In the upper right background, General George A. Custer can be seen with his staff, still reveling in the victory and displaying banners captured from the Confederates in an earlier victory.

MARSHALL'S CROSSROADS

30" X 44"

The Surrender

After four bloody and exhausting years of fratricidal war, the two main armies of the Union and Confederacy converged upon the little town of Appomattox Court House in Appomattox County, Virginia. Lieutenant General Ulysses S. Grant had finally been able to cut General Robert E. Lee and the Army of Northern Virginia off from their supply trains after relentlessly pursuing Lee's army from Petersburg and Richmond. A series of engagements in the first week of April had all but finished the Army of Northern Virginia. A final battle loomed, the outcome of which was a foregone conclusion.

Lee, though used to being heavily outnumbered, was forced to face a damning choice. He could fight a pointless battle and lose many of his stoutest veterans; he could disband the army and have the men scatter to the hills to fight on as guerrillas; or, he could surrender to Grant and seek honorable terms. After consulting with his remaining commanders, Lee decided to seek terms, bitterly admitting that he "would rather die a thousand deaths."

Grant, for his part, was riding through the muddy roads, trying to make sure that Lee had no chance for escape. The pressure had given Grant a severe headache, which vanished when a courier overtook him and presented him with a message from Lee, asking to meet to discuss terms for surrender. Grant wasted no time in making his way to the home of Wilmer McLean, the closest suitable place for the event.

The two commanders and their chosen staff met in the parlor of McLean's farm house. McLean had moved to the quiet little village to escape the ravages of war, which wreaked havoc on his home at Manassas, Virginia in the summer of 1861. Now the war had followed him into the sanctity of his front parlor. McLean would later boast that the Civil War started in his front yard, and ended in his parlor.

Lee prepared himself for the meeting by dressing himself in formal uniform with sword and sash. Grant, for his part, did not pay attention to such niceties and rode up in his mud spattered field uniform, an unadorned private's blouse with shoulder boards. According to Grant, "When I went into the house I found General Lee. We greeted each other, and after shaking hands, took our seats. I had my staff with me, a good portion of whom were in the room during the whole of the interview." In fact, Grant seemed embarrassed by the circumstances, and conversed with Lee about the Mexican War. Grant remembered Lee, who was a prominent member of

Winfield Scott's staff. Lee did not recall Grant, who had been an obscure lieutenant at the time. Lee had to prod Grant to get the discussion on track.

Grant discussed the matter with Lee and wrote down terms. Officers were allowed to keep their side-arms. Enlisted men would surrender their arms and be paroled. Grant provided rations for Lee's men and allowed those with horses to keep them, a very generous clause he added when Lee informed him that unlike the Union army Confederate officers and cavalry provided their own mounts. It was a solemn, simple ending to the bloody conflict between these two great armies. The end was cordial, and even friendly. All rose in silence and followed the generals outside, where Lee was saluted by all of the Federal officers as he took his departure.

Afterwards Grant's staff deluged McLean with offers to buy his furniture and other items as souvenirs of the historic moment. Some items were bought, but almost everything was taken, paid for or otherwise. When the Union soldiers began cheering at news of the surrender, Grant ordered it to cease, the rebels were their countrymen again.

This dramatic painting captures the drama and poignancy of the moment, as Grant and Lee shake hands after the surrender. Every detail is painstakingly recreated, from the patterned rug on the floor to the rag doll on the mantle, the "silent witness." Lee is accompanied only by Colonel Charles Marshall, who looks over the terms with Ely Parker, a Seneca Indian. The spectators, Grant's staff officers, stand around the room in respectful silence, drinking in every moment of this historic event for which they had fought so long and hard. Captain Robert Todd Lincoln, son of the president, holds Grant's chair. Philip Sheridan is seated behind Lincoln, leaning forward.

THE SURRENDER

BIBLIOGRAPHY

Acken, J. Gregory, editor, Inside the Army of the Potomac: The Civil War experience of Captian Francis Adams Donaldson, (Stackpole Books, Mechanicsburg, 1998).

Adkin, Mark, The Gettysburg Companion, (Stackpole Books, Mechanicsburg, 2008).

Archer, John M., Culp's Hill at Gettysburg, (Thomas Publications, Gettysburg, 2002).

Barber, Lucius, Army Memoirs, (J.M.W. Jones Stationary and printing Co., Chicago, 1894)

Booth, George W., A Maryland Boy in Lee's Army, (University of Nebraska Press, Lincoln, 2000).

Buel, Clarence C. and Robert U. Johnson, editors. Battle and Leaders of the Civil War, four volumes, (The Century Co, New York, 1884-1888)

Burchard, Peter, One Gallant Rush, (St. Martin's Press, New York, 1965)

Butterfield, Daniel, Camp and Outpost Duty for Infantry, (Harper & Brothers, New York, 1862).

Child, William, A History of the Fifth Regiment New Hampshire Volunteers in the American Civil War, 1861-1865, (R.W. Musgrove, Bristol, 1893).

Coates, Earl J., Michael J. McAfee , and Don Troiani, Don Troiani's Regiments and Uniforms of the Civil War, (Stackpole Books, Mechanicsville, 2002).

Cockrell, Monroe F., editor, The Lost Account of the Battle of Corinth and the Court Martial of Gen. Van Dorn, (Broadfoot Publishing Co., Wilmington, 1991)

Coddington, Edwin B., The Gettysburg Campaign: A Study in Command, (Charles Scribner's Sons, New York, 1968)

Coggins, Jack, Arms and Equipment of the Civil War, (The Fairfax Press, New York, 1983)

Cox, John D., Culp's Hill: The Attack and Defense of the Union Flank July 2, 1863, (Da Capo Press, Cambridge, 2004).

Cozzens, Peter, The Darkest Days of the War: The Battles of Iuka and Corinth, (University of North Carolina Press, Chapel Hill, 1997)

Crawford, J. Marshall, Mosby and His Men, (G.W. Carleton and Co., New York, 1867).

Cullen, Joseph P., The Peninsula Campaign of 1862, (Bonanza Nooks, New York, 1973).

Davis, Burke, The Long Surrender, (Random House, New York, 1985).

Davis, William C., First Blood: Fort Sumter to Bull Run, (Time-Life Books, Alexandria, 1983).

Davis, William C., The Image of War, Volume One, Shadows of the Storm, (Doubleday and Co., Garden City, 1981).

Dawes, Rufus B., Service with the Sixth Wisconsin, (Morningside Bookshop, Dayton, 1984)

Drury, Ian and Tony Gibbons, The Civil War Military Machine, (Dragon's World, Ltd., London, 1993).

Dufour, Charles, Gentle Tiger: The Gallant Life of Roberdeau Wheat, (Louisiana State University Press, Baton Rouge, 1957).

Eby, Henry H., Observations of an Illinois Boy in Battle, Camp and Prisons, 1861-1865, (Mendota, 1910)

Elting, John R., Military Uniforms in America Volume III: Long Endure, The Civil War Period 1852-1867, (Presidio Press, Novato, 1982).

Folsom, James M., Heroes and Martyrs of Georgia, (Burke, Boykin & Co., Macon, 1864).

Fox, William F., Regimental Losses in the American Civil War 1861-1865, (Brandow Printing Co., Albany, 1898).

Gallagher, Gary, editor, The Richmond Campaign of 1862: The peninsula and the Seven Days, (University of North Carolina Press, Chapel Hill, 2000).

Garafolo, Robert and Mark Elrod, A Pictorial History of Civil War Era Musical Instruments and Military Bands, (Pictorial Histories Publishing Co., Charleston, 1985).

Giles, Valerius, Rags and Hope, The Recollections of Val C. Giles, Four Years with Hood's Brigade, Fourth Texas Infantry, 1861-1865, (Coward-McCann, New York, 1961).

Girardi, Robert I., The Soldier's View: The Civil War Art of Keith Rocco, (Military History Press, Berkeley, 2004)

Goldsborough, W.W., The Maryland Line in the Confederate Army, 1861-1865, (Guggenheimer Weil and Co., Maryland, 1900).

Grossman, Julian, The Civil War: Battlefields and Campgrounds in the Art of Winslow Homer, (Abradale Press, New York, 1991)

Halsey, Ashley, editor, A Yankee Private's Civil War, (Henry Regnery Co., Chicago, 1961)

Heaps, Willard A. and Porter W., The Singing Sixties, (University of Oklahoma Press, Norman, 1960).

Hess, Earl J., Pickett's Charge-The Last Attack at Gettysburg, (University of North Carolina Press, Chapel Hill, 2001).

Hutton, Joseph, History of the 2nd West Virginia Cavalry, (Blue Acorn Press, Huntington, 1993)

Hyndman, William, History of a Cavalry Company, (Jas. B. Rodgers Co., Philadelphia, 1870).

Jones, Terry L., Lee's Tigers: The Louisiana Infantry in the Army of Northern Virginia, (Louisiana State University Press, Baton Rouge, 1987).

Kautz, August V., The 1863 Customs of Service for Non-commissioned Officers and Soldiers, (J.B. Lippincott and Co., Philadelphia, 1864)

Lord, Francis A., They Fought for the Union, (Bonanza Books, New York, 1960).

Lord, Francis, A Civil War Collector's Encyclopedia, (Castle Books, New Jersey, 1982)
Madden, James M., The History of the Fighting Fourteenth, (Butternut and Blue, Baltimore, 1994).

Mahan, Dennis H., An Elementary Treatise on Advanced Guard, Outpost and Detachment of Troops and the Manner of Posting and Handling Them in the Presence of an Enemy, (John Wiley, New York, 1862)

Marvel, William, A Place Called Appomattox, (University of North Carolina Press, Chapel Hill, 2000).

McCarthy, Carlton, Detailed Minutiae of Soldier Life, (Carlton McCarthy and Co, Richmond, 1882)

McElfresh, Earl B., Maps and mapmakers of the Civil War, (Harry N. Abrams, Inc., New York, 1999).

McKim, Randolph H., A Soldier's Recollections, (Longman's Green & Co., London, 1910)

McLean, James L., Cutler's Brigade at Gettysburg, (Butternut and Blue, Baltimore, 1994).

McPherson, James, Battle Cry of Freedom, (Oxford University Press, New York, 1988)

Mosby, John S., edited by Charles Wells Russell, The Memoirs of Colonel John S. Mosby, (Little Brown & Co, Boston, 1917).

Norton, Oliver W., The Attack and Defense of Little Round Top, (Morningside Bookshop, Dayton, 1983).

Pfanz, Harry W., Gettysburg, the Second Day, (University of North Carolina Press, Chapel Hill, 1987).

Pfanz, Harry W., Gettysburg: Culp's Hill & Cemetery Hill, (University of North Carolina Press, Chape Hill, 1993)

Pfanz, Harry W., Gettysburg—the First Day, (University of North Carolina Press, Chapel Hill, 2001).

Polley, J.B., Hood's Texas Brigade: Its Marches, Its Battles, Its Achievements, (Neale, New York, 1910).

Pride, Mark and Mark Travis, My Brave Boys: To War with Colonel Cross and the Fighting Fifth, {University Press of New England, Hanover, 2001).

Pullen, John J., The Twentieth Maine, (J.B. Lippincott and Co., Philadelphia, 1957)

Rhea, Gordon, The Battle of the Wilderness, (Louisiana State University Press, Baton Rouge, 1998).

Rice, Ralsa, Yankee Tigers: Through the Civil War with the 125th Ohio, (Blue Acorn Press, Huntington, 1992)

Robertson, James I., Soldiers Blue and Gray, (University of South Carolina press, Columbia, 1988)

Sears, Stephen, Landscape Turned Red: The Battle of Antietam, (Ticknor & Fields, New Haven, 1983)

Smith, Raymond W., Out of the Wilderness: The Civil War Memoir of Cpl. Norton C. Shepard, 146th New York Volunteer Infantry, (Edmonston Publishing Inc., New York, 1998).

Smith, Robin and Bill Younghusband, American Civil War Zouaves, (Osprey Publishing, Oxford, 1996).

Smith, Robin and Ron Field, Uniforms of the Civil War, (The Lyons Press, Guilford, 2001).

Stillwell, Leander, The Story of a Common Soldier, (Hudson Publishing Co., Franklin, 1920)

Tevis, C.V. and D.R. Marquis, compilers, The History of the Fighting 14th, (Butternut & Blue, Baltimore, 1994)

Todd, Frederick P., American Military Equipage 1851-1872, Volume II, (Chatham Square Press, 1983).

Trulock, Alice R., In the Hands of Providence: Joshua L. Chamberlain and the American Civil War, (University of North Carolina Press, Chapel Hill, 1992)

U.S. War Department, Revised Regulations for the Army of the Unite States, 1861, (J.G.L. Brown, Philadelphia, 1861)

U.S. War Department, The War of the Rebellion: A Compendium of the Official Records of the Union and Confederate Armies, 127 volumes (GPO, Washington, D.C., 1880-1901).

Waite, Otis R., New Hampshire in the Great Rebellion, (Tracy, Chase and Co., Claremont, 1870).

Keith Rocco's passion for history and art began at an early age when he talked his parents into getting him The Golden Book of the Civil War for Christmas. The book inspired the budding, young artist to meticulously copy the pictures. At age 14 he began what today has become a solid collection of Civil War and Napoleonic artifacts along with an eclectic mix of costuming from a variety of periods, "There is no better way to achieve an insight into a period and its people than by holding an artifact in your hands. For the artist, if you don't know the grade of cloth used on a garment you can't understand how it will hang or fold. It is the manufacturing processes and available materials of a period that are most crucial to recreating the essence of an era." says Rocco.

Because he never puts brush to canvas without exhaustive research, he finds he must begin his planning months and occasionally years before he may start a painting. The result of all this research and work has been gold for Rocco's art. In 1985 Rocco was proclaimed by the French magazine Uniformes, as an "artist in the tradition of Remington and Detaille." His works currently hang in every major collection of historical art in the country and several abroad. These include the Andrew Mellon Foundation, the Pentagon, the Atlanta Historical Society, the House of Representatives, Gettysburg National Park, the City of Fredericksburg, Virginia, the National Guard Heritage Collection, the U.S. Army War College and numerous private collections. In 2003, he designed the centerpiece mural "Gettysburg", for the Abraham Lincoln Presidential Library and Museum in Springfield, Illinois.

Rocco's paintings have been displayed in special exhibits across the country, including the 1992 Birth of a Nation exhibition in Washington, D.C., and a one man show entitled On Campaign at the Cyclorama Building in Gettysburg National Park in 1994. His painterly and fluid style and extensive research of his subject has made Rocco one of the nation's most respected narrative artists.

Originally from Illinois, today Keith Rocco lives and paints in Virginia's Shenandoah Valley.

Robert I. Girardi has had a life long fascination with the Civil War. He has studied the war from all sides, and has tramped over many of the battlefields and related sites. He has collected artifacts and memorabilia and has read through thousands of documents and letters written by participants. In this manner, he has developed a sense of what the soldiers experienced. He has become an author and historian in his own right and has become a popular speaker and consultant on the American Civil War to audiences of all ages. Robert created a Civil War exhibit for the Bureau County Historical Society in Princeton, Illinois, using local artifacts. He has spoken to historical societies and Civil War groups all over the United States and is a well known authority on the subject in the Chicago area where he has been interviewed on both radio and television on aspects of the Civil War.

Robert earned his M.A. in Public History at Loyola University of Chicago in 1991. He is a past president of the Civil War Round Table of Chicago and is currently vice president of the Salt Creek Civil War Round Table. He belongs to two other Civil War round tables in the Chicago area. He is a fellow of the Company of Military Historians and is an associate member of the Sons of Union Veterans. He is on the editorial review board of the Journal of the Illinois State Historical Society and has consulted for the Chicago Historical Society on its Civil War exhibits.

Robert I. Girardi has authored or edited six previous books: Campaigning with Uncle Billy: The Civil War Memoirs of Sgt. Lyman S. Widney, 34th Illinois Volunteer Infantry, The Soldier's View: The Civil War Art of Keith Rocco, The New Annals of the Civil War, The Memoirs of Brigadier General William Passmore Carlin, U.S.A., The Military Memoirs of General John Pope and Captain H.W. Chester: Recollections of the War of the Rebellion.

Robert I. Girardi lives and works in Chicago where he is employed as a homicide detective by the Chicago Police Department.